Earth's Rivers

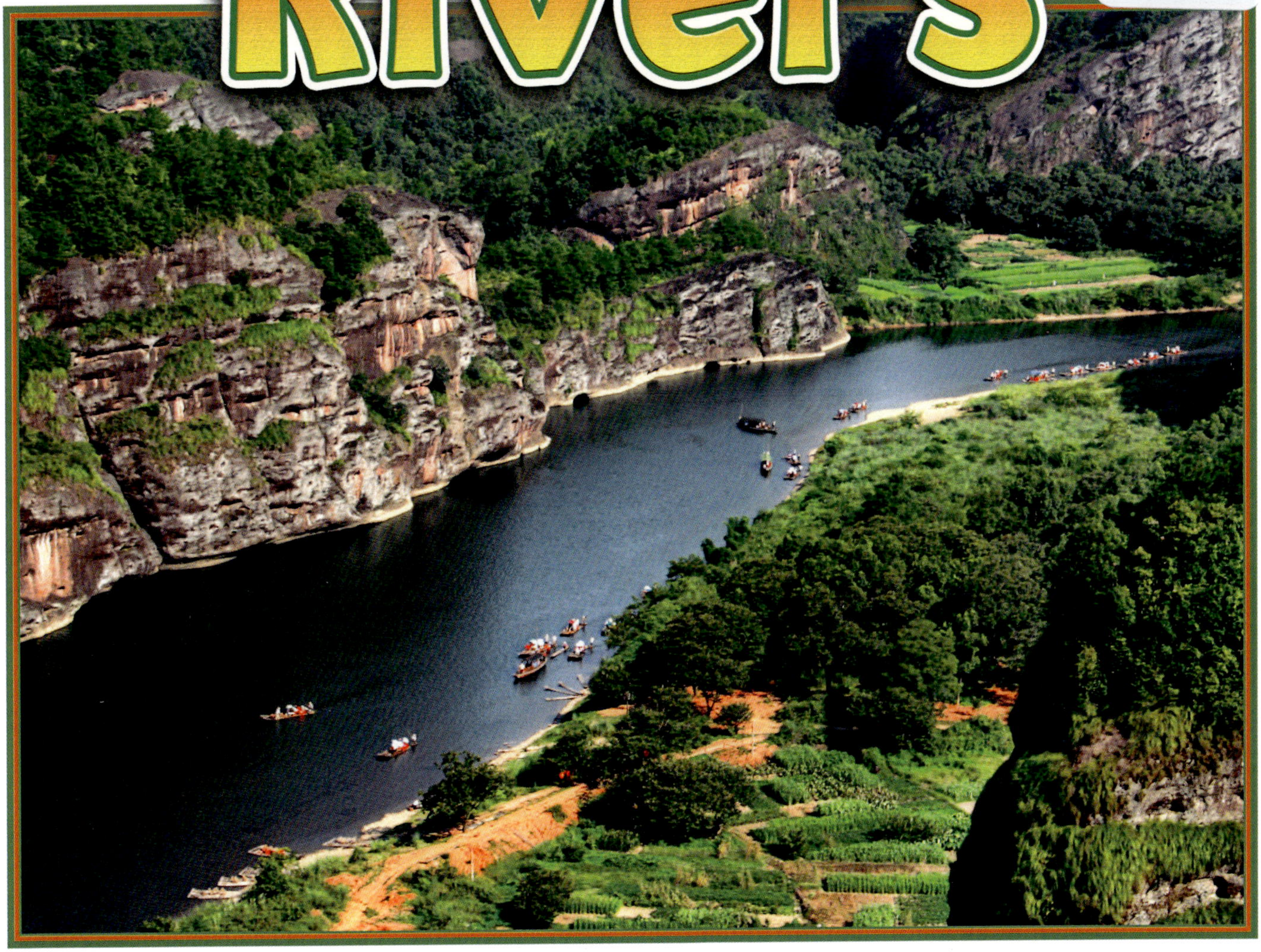

Bobbie Kalman

Crabtree Publishing Company

www.crabtreebooks.com

Created by Bobbie Kalman

For Bev, with whom I shared my first trip back to Budapest
I'll never forget our years of fun in Nassau and Europe!

Author and Editor-in-Chief
Bobbie Kalman

Research
Robin Johnson

Editor
Kathy Middleton

Photo research
Bobbie Kalman
Crystal Sikkens

Design
Bobbie Kalman
Katherine Berti
Samantha Crabtree (cover)

Production coordinator
Katherine Berti

Prepress technician
Margaret Amy Salter

Consultant
Joel Mercer,
former Head of the Geography Department,
Galt Collegiate Institute

Illustrations
Barbara Bedell: page 15
Katherine Kantor: pages 7, 9, 22
Jeannette McNaughton-Julich: page 19

Photographs
© Dreamstime.com: pages 5 (bottom), 19 (bottom), 21 (bottom left), 24 (top left), 25 (top), 27 (top)
© iStockphoto.com: page 23 (top except inset)
© Shutterstock.com: front and back cover, title page, pages 3, 4, 5 (top), 6, 7, 8, 9, 10, 11, 12, 13, 14, 15, 16, 17, 18, 19 (top), 20, 21 (except bottom left), 22, 23 (inset and bottom), 24 (bottom), 25 (bottom), 26, 27 (bottom), 28 (bottom left), 29 (bottom), 30, 31
Other images by Digital Vision

Library and Archives Canada Cataloguing in Publication

Kalman, Bobbie, 1947-
Earth's rivers / Bobbie Kalman.

(Looking at earth)
Includes index.
ISBN 978-0-7787-3208-2 (bound).--ISBN 978-0-7787-3218-1 (pbk.)

1. Rivers--Juvenile literature. I. Title. II. Series.

GB1203.8.K34 2008 j551.48'3 C2008-905548-9

Library of Congress Cataloging-in-Publication Data

Kalman, Bobbie.
Earth's rivers / Bobbie Kalman.
p. cm. -- (Looking at earth)
Includes index.
ISBN-13: 978-0-7787-3218-1 (pbk. : alk. paper)
ISBN-10: 0-7787-3218-5 (pbk. : alk. paper)
ISBN-13: 978-0-7787-3208-2 (reinforced library binding : alk. paper)
ISBN-10: 0-7787-3208-8 (reinforced library binding : alk. paper)
1. Rivers--Juvenile literature. I. Title. II. Series.

GB1203.8.K35 2009
551.48'3--dc22
2008035386

Crabtree Publishing Company
www.crabtreebooks.com 1-800-387-7650

Printed in the USA/082018/PS20180705

Copyright © **2009 CRABTREE PUBLISHING COMPANY**. All rights reserved. No part of this publication may be reproduced, stored in a retrieval system or be transmitted in any form or by any means, electronic, mechanical, photocopying, recording, or otherwise, without the prior written permission of Crabtree Publishing Company. In Canada: We acknowledge the financial support of the Government of Canada through the Canada Book Fund for our publishing activities.

Published in Canada
Crabtree Publishing
616 Welland Ave.
St. Catharines, Ontario
L2M 5V6

Published in the United States Crabtree Publishing
PMB 59051
350 Fifth Avenue, 59th Floor
New York, New York 10118

Published in the United Kingdom
Crabtree Publishing
Maritime House
Basin Road North, Hove
BN41 1WR

Published in Australia
Crabtree Publishing
3 Charles Street
Coburg North
VIC, 3058

Contents

This girl is carrying water from a river to her home.

What is a river?

A **river** is a body of water that moves from one place to another. Rivers usually flow from higher places to lower places. As they flow, they carry **fresh water** to plants, animals, and people. Fresh water does not contain a lot of salt. Rivers also move and shape the land. There are some very big rivers on Earth. Which river is closest to your home?

*These children are standing on a **bank** of a river. A bank is a side of a river. A deer has come to the river to drink water. Many animals find water and food in rivers.*

The plants in the water above are growing on the river ***bed****. A bed is the bottom of a river.*

Rivers flow in ***channels****. Channels are grooves in the land created by rivers. This picture shows a river from an airplane. The river runs in a channel in the ground.*

From source to mouth

The **source** of a river is where it begins. The **mouth** is where it ends. Rivers change as they flow from source to mouth. Many rivers are steep and narrow at the source. They flow quickly and roughly down mountains. They rush over bumpy **rapids**. Rapids are shallow, rocky parts of rivers where the **currents** are very strong and fast. Some rivers drop over steep rocks at **waterfalls**.

These children are rafting through some very bumpy rapids on a river.

Winding down

As rivers travel, they become wider and less steep than they were near their sources. They wind slowly over the land in large curves and bends called **meanders**.

Headwaters *are small streams that flow together to form a river. These streams have become part of a river.*

A ***tributary*** *is a small river that flows into a larger river.*

Rivers and lakes

The water near a river's source is clean. As it flows, it picks up ***silt****. Silt is made up of tiny pieces of rock or soil.*

Most rivers begin high on hills or **mountains**. A mountain is a very tall and steep area of rocky land. Some mountains have **glaciers** on them. A glacier is a huge, slow-moving body of ice. When glaciers melt, water runs down the mountains as rivers. Rain and snow also become part of river water.

The end

Rivers flow downhill across the land. Eventually, most rivers end when they reach an **ocean** or a **lake**. An ocean is a huge area of **salt water**. A lake is a large body of fresh water with land all around it.

Earth's biggest lake

Many rivers flow into lakes. Lake Baikal in Russia is the oldest lake in the world! It is also the deepest and biggest lake. Six big rivers and more than 330 small rivers flow into Lake Baikal. The rivers start in the mountains around the lake.

The Great Lakes

The Great Lakes are Lake Superior, Lake Huron, Lake Erie, Lake Ontario, and Lake Michigan. Four of the lakes are on the border of Canada and the United States. Lake Michigan is only in the United States.

The Great Lakes are connected to one another by rivers and **canals**. Canals are human-made waterways. The St. Lawrence Seaway is the name of the system of canals and **locks** that connects the Great Lakes to the Atlantic Ocean. It is shown on this map.

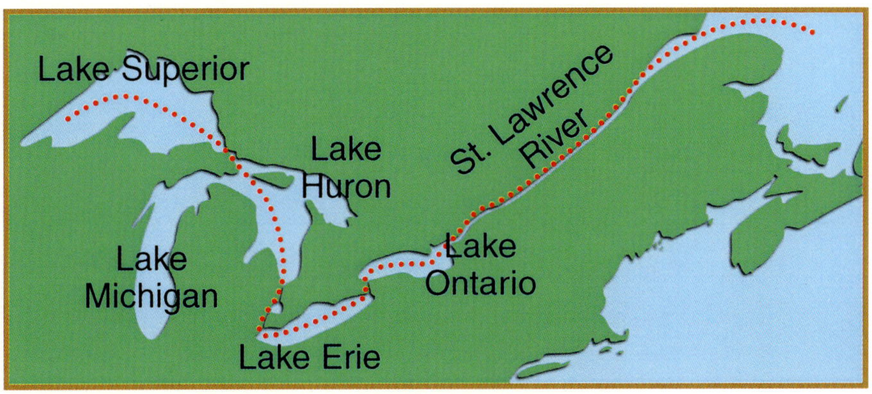

The St. Lawrence Seaway allows huge ships to travel from the Atlantic Ocean to the Great Lakes. The seaway is shown by the red dotted line. After which river is it named?

Flowing into oceans

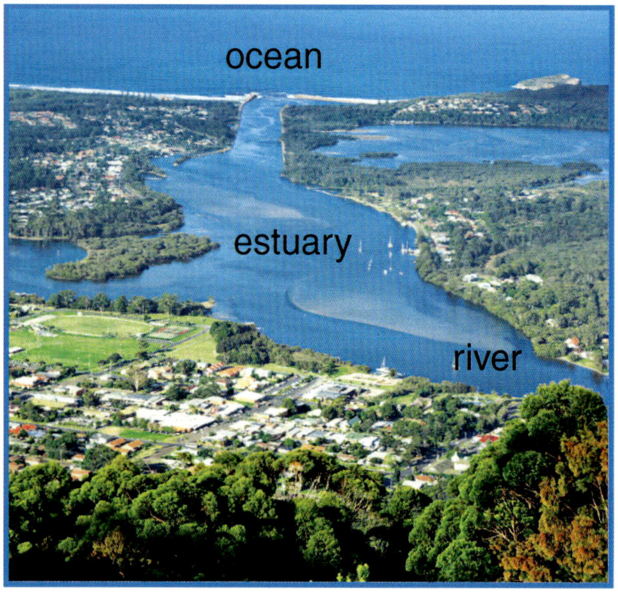

At the end of their journeys, rivers flow gently over flat land to their mouths. At their mouths, some rivers become parts of oceans. Rivers that flow into oceans may form **estuaries**. Estuaries are areas that contain **brackish** water. Brackish water contains both fresh water from a river and salt water from an ocean.

Estuaries are home to many plants and animals. Birds visit estuaries to find food.

River deltas

Some rivers create **deltas** when they reach oceans or lakes. A delta is a large muddy area at a river's mouth, where the river splits into many channels. Deltas are made up of the soil and sand that rivers **deposit** at their mouths. Many deltas are shaped like triangles.

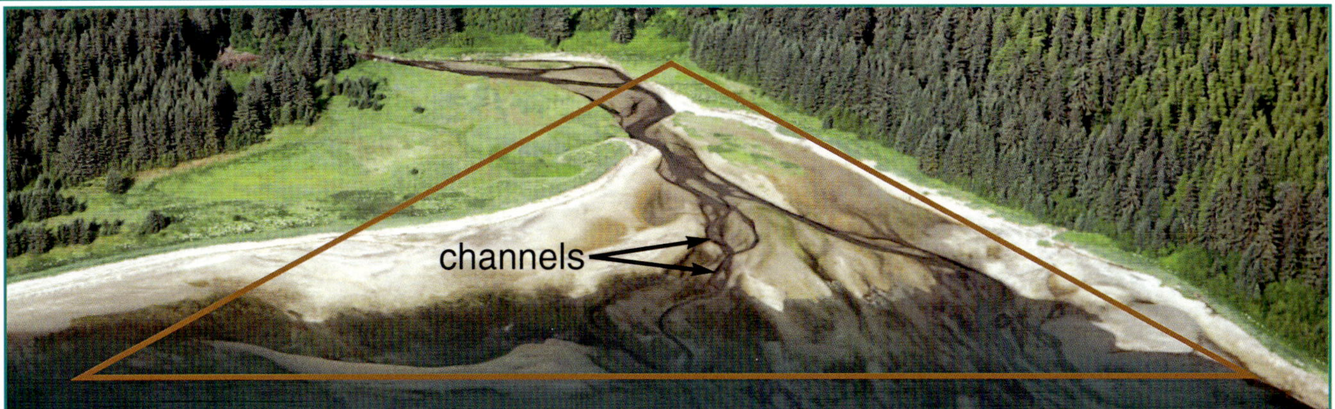

This delta is seen from above. It has a triangle shape.

Soil that the river carried and deposited created the land between these channels.

Plants grow well in delta soil. These horses find plenty of grasses to eat on a river delta.

Shaping the land

Rivers carry cold, fresh water down from mountains. They also carry rocks, stones, dirt, and sand that they pick up along the way.

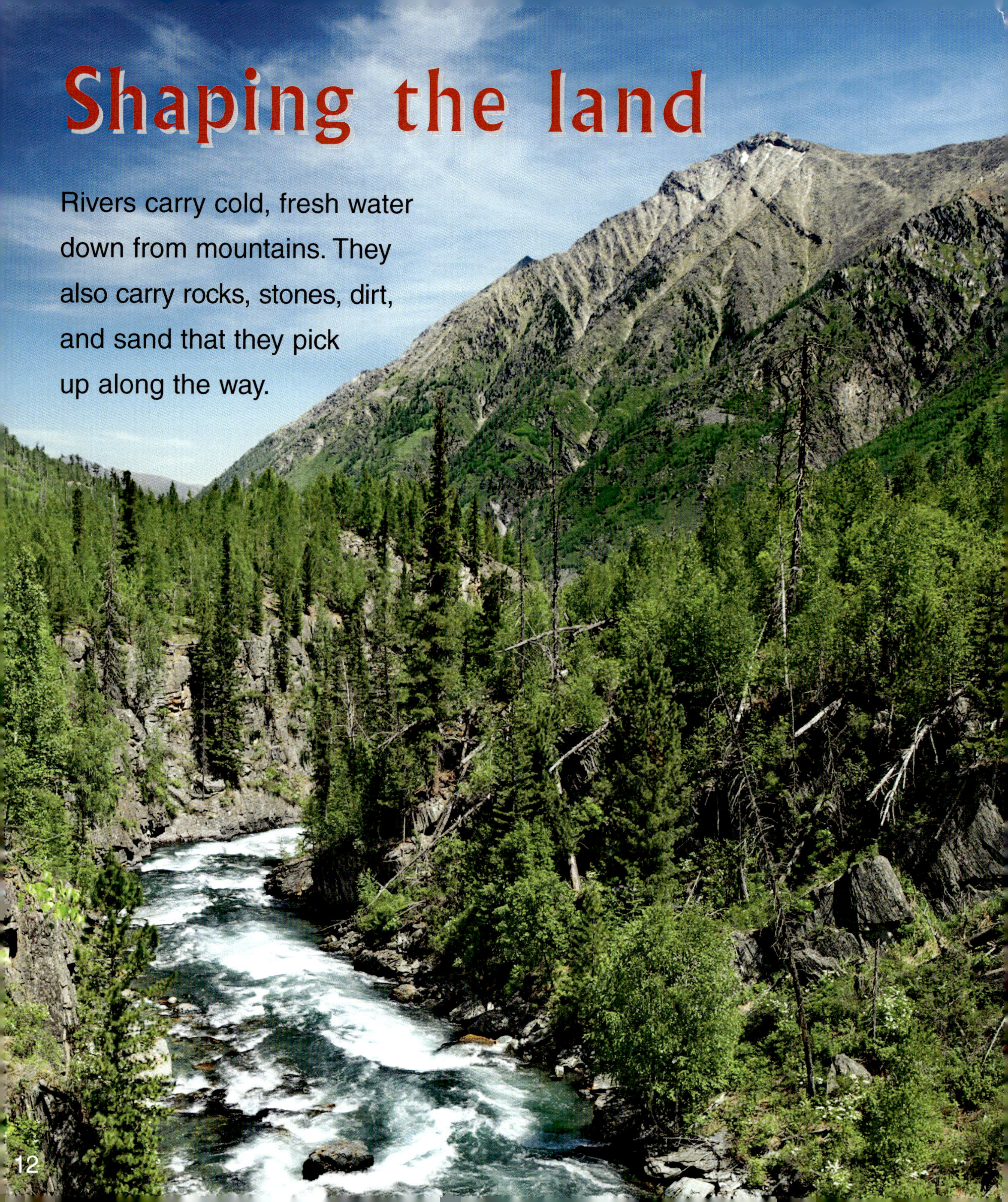

Wearing away

The rocks carried by rivers bounce and bump along the bottom and sides of the rivers. They break off pieces of land. Over time, the land around rivers becomes **eroded**. Eroded means worn away.

These rocks have been carried by this river.

Canyons and valleys

Some rivers **carve**, or cut, **valleys** into the land. A valley is a low area of land between higher land. Some rivers carve huge **canyons**. A canyon is a deep valley with steep sides.

The Colorado River carved the Grand Canyon.

Underground caves

Some rivers flow under the ground and can create **caves**. Caves are open areas under the Earth. An underground river in Mexico winds through 95 miles (153 km) of caves.

This cave has a river running through it.

Part of the water cycle

Rivers end when they reach oceans and lakes, but the water that they carry never stops moving. It is part of the **water cycle**. The water cycle is the movement of water into the sky and back down to Earth. Water moves into the sky as **water vapor**. Water vapor is a gas in the air. Water falls back down to Earth as rain or snow.

You can see the fog among the trees above. The water droplets in fog and mist turn into water vapor and rise high into the air.

The water in a river is liquid water.

Changing and moving

Rising warm air carries the water vapor up into the sky. High in the sky, the vapor cools and forms clouds. Water falls from clouds as rain or snow. It falls into rivers. Some water soaks into soil and between rocks and becomes **ground water**. Ground water also flows into rivers. Rivers carry the rain, melted snow, and ground water to lakes and oceans.

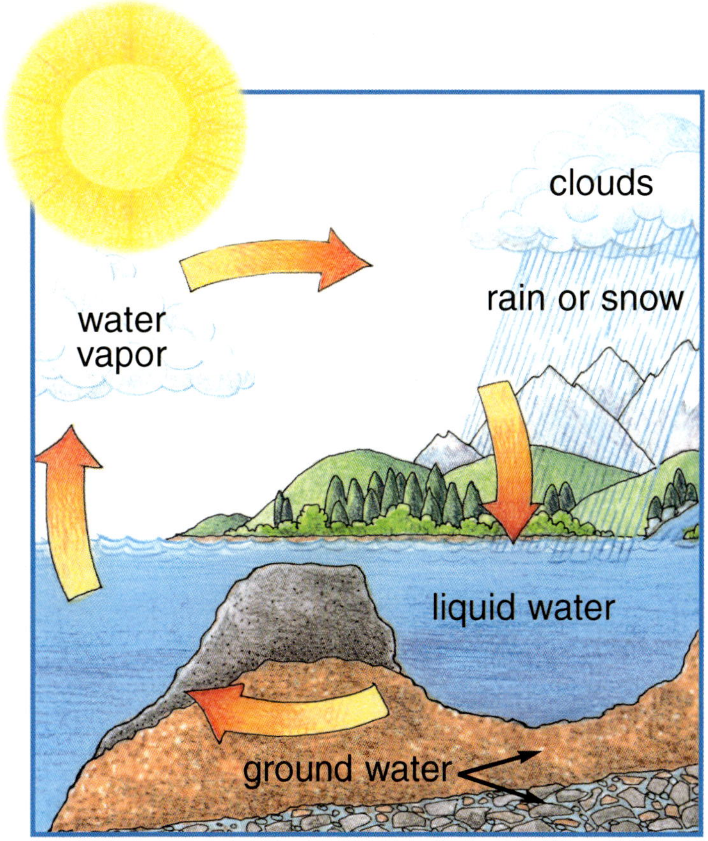

Ground water is in soil or among rocks.

The sun melts ice and snow on mountaintops. The ice and snow change to liquid water. The water runs down into rivers and then into lakes.

Water for living things

The roots of these trees get water from a river.

All living things need water. They need water to live, grow, and stay healthy. Plants take in water through their **roots**. Roots are the parts of plants that are under the ground or under water. Many plants grow in or beside rivers.

Water for animals

Animals that live on land need water, too. They need to drink fresh water. Fresh water does not have a lot of salt in it and is safe to drink.

Water for people

Rivers bring fresh water to people, too. Water from rivers is brought into homes through pipes and taps. The water is cleaned first.

Rivers bring cool water to thirsty animals. These elephants are drinking water in a river. They are also using the water to bathe and to cool themselves.

This girl is drinking water from a tap in a park. The water came from a river.

*Farmers use water from rivers to spray their **crops**. Crops are plants grown as food.*

River habitats

Many animals live in river **habitats**. Habitats are the natural places where animals live. Many types of fish live only in freshwater rivers and lakes. Other animals, such as frogs, turtles, and ducks, live in rivers and along the banks of rivers. Other animals visit rivers to cool their bodies, to find food to eat, and to drink fresh water.

This bear caught a salmon in a river.

Some turtles and frogs live in rivers. They find food to eat in the water and on river banks.

Building dams

Beavers build **dams** in rivers and streams. Beaver dams are walls made of logs, sticks, and mud. Beavers build dams to slow down river waters and create deep **ponds**. Ponds are small lakes with still waters. Beavers build their homes in the ponds.

*A beaver's home is called a **lodge**.*

Beavers have worked hard to build this dam. They will build their lodge in the pond.

People and rivers

People build dams, too. They build big, strong dams across rivers to control how rivers flow. Some dams are used to create **reservoirs**, or human-made lakes. People in towns and cities get their fresh water from reservoirs. Other dams are used to make **hydroelectricity**. Hydroelectricity is power created from falling water. List all the ways you use electricity in your home.

This dam is creating a large reservoir of fresh water. It is also used to make hydroelectricity.

River boats

People travel and carry goods on rivers. They use boats to get from place to place. **Barges** are boats that **transport**, or carry, goods along big rivers. **Ferries** carry people, cars, and goods along or across rivers. Rafts, canoes, and other small boats are used for travel, sports, and fun.

This boy is learning to paddle a kayak.

The people in this houseboat can travel without leaving their home.

This barge is carrying goods down the Mississippi River.

This woman is selling fruit and vegetables from her boat.

This ferry carries cars and people.

Earth's longest rivers

Rivers are found on every **continent** except Antarctica. A continent is a huge area of land. The continents that have rivers are: North America, South America, Europe, Africa, Asia, and Australia and Oceania. Some of the world's longest rivers are shown on the map below.

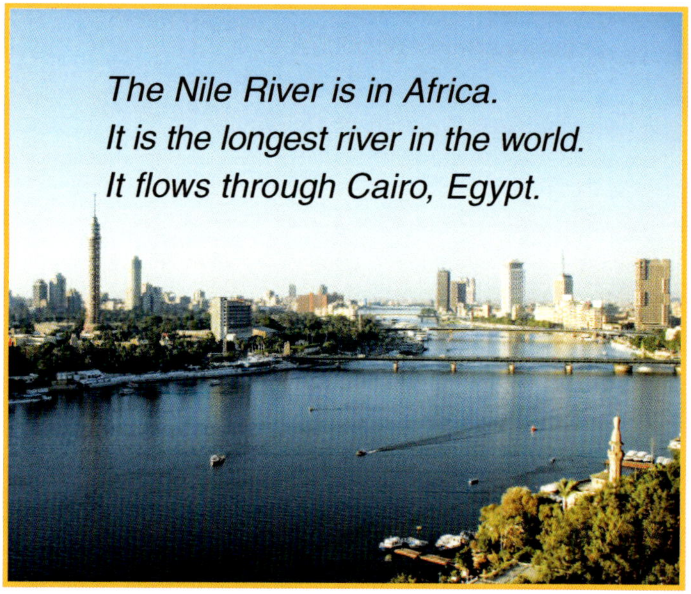

The Nile River is in Africa. It is the longest river in the world. It flows through Cairo, Egypt.

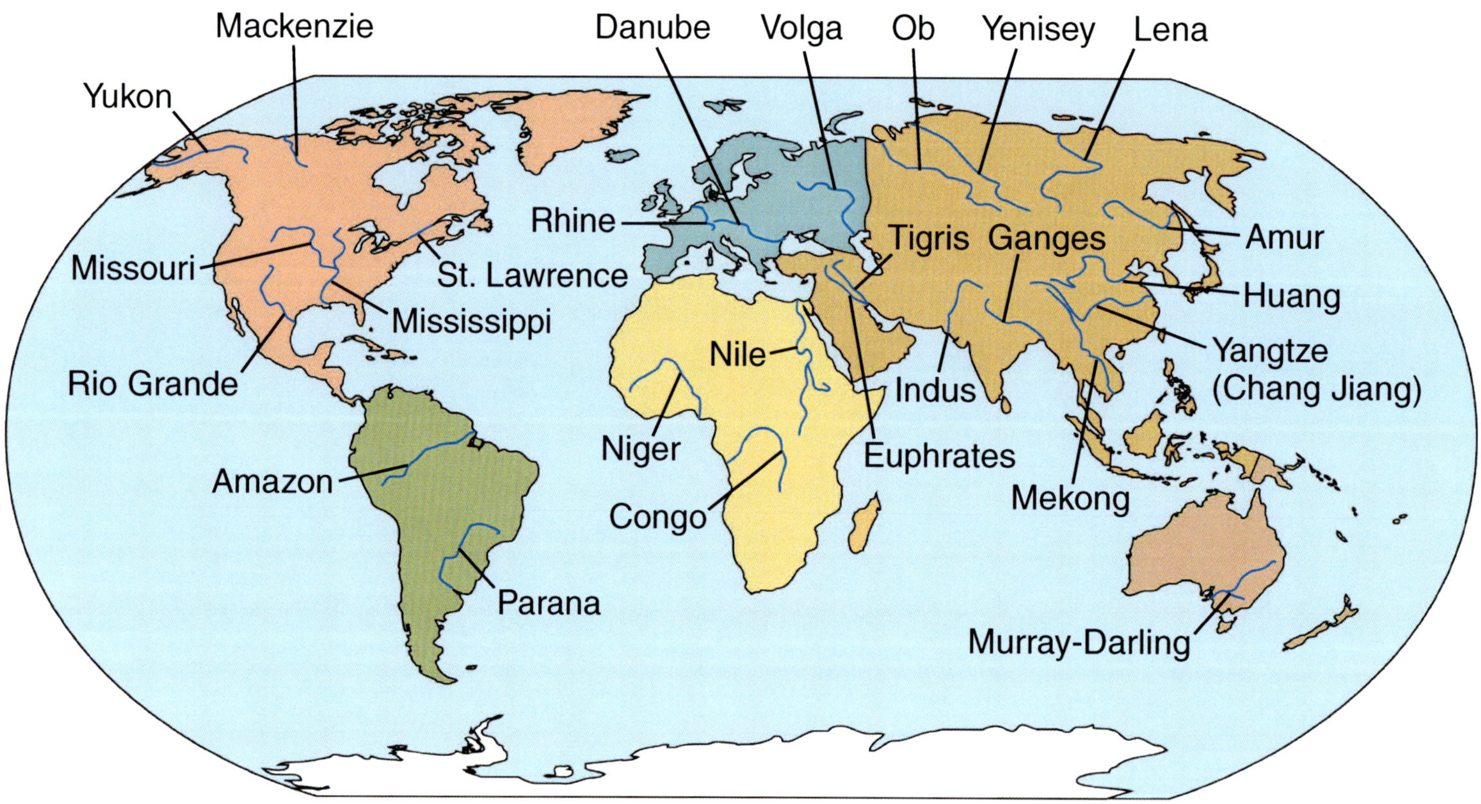

The largest river

The Amazon River is in South America. It is the second-longest river in the world, but it is the largest. It carries about one-fifth of the world's river water! Millions of kinds of plants and animals live in this amazing river and in the Amazon **Rain Forest**. The Amazon River flows through this huge forest.

This monkey lives in the Amazon Rain Forest.

Amazon River

The Yangtze River in China is the longest river in Asia. It is the third-longest river in the world. This man is fishing on the Yangtze River.

More big rivers

Nizhny Novgorod is a Russian city on the Volga River, where it meets the Oka River.

Europe's longest river is the Volga. The Volga River is in Russia. Europe's second-longest river is the Danube. It flows through some of Europe's most beautiful cities, such as Vienna and Budapest. Australia's longest river is the Murray-Darling.

This city is Budapest, Hungary's capital city. It is on the banks of the Danube River.

The Murray-Darling Basin is made up of the Murray and Darling rivers. Together, the two rivers make up the longest river in Australia.

The Missouri River is the longest river in North America. It is a tributary of the Mississippi River, the second-longest river. This old riverboat is on the Mississippi. It takes people on tours along this river.

The Yukon River is in Alaska and in northwest Canada. It is the fourth-longest river in North America.

The St. Lawrence River connects the Great Lakes with the Atlantic Ocean. It is a very important river. This picture shows the river in front of the city of Montreal.

Too dry or too wet?

These elephants have gone to a river to get a drink. They are digging into the sand to find water, but the water has dried up.

Farmers need flooded fields for growing rice plants.

Most of the world's rivers carry water all year long, but some rivers dry up for part of the year. Rivers dry up during **droughts**. Droughts are long periods of time with little or no rain. When rivers dry up, it is hard for people, animals, and plants to get the water they need.

Rising waters

Other rivers can have too much water. When there is too much water in rivers, the rivers overflow and cause **floods**. Floods are huge amounts of water that cover the land. Heavy rain or snow that melts too quickly sometimes causes floods. Floods can make land more **fertile** for farming, but floods also cause a lot of damage to buildings, cars, and land areas.

*A **floodplain** is an area of flat land beside a river. It is often covered with flood water. The water carries silt onto the land. Silt makes floodplains good for growing crops.*

Some flooding helps people, but most floods are disasters. People lose their homes, cars, and even families. In 2008, seven states in the United States were flooded when rivers overflowed their banks.

***Global warming** may be the cause of some floods. As the Earth heats up, more ice melts at the North and South poles. This water gets added to rivers. Rivers fill up and flood the land.*

Protecting our rivers

Rivers are important to all living things, but many rivers are no longer safe. Rivers around the world have become **polluted**, or dirty. When rivers are polluted, animals and plants can no longer live in them. The water in the rivers cannot be used for drinking. Without fresh water to drink, living things cannot stay alive. Many fish that swim in polluted rivers die.

Factories are often built near rivers. They use river water to make their products. Many factories dump ***chemicals*** *back into the rivers. Chemicals are poisons that are dangerous to living things.*

People spray ***pesticides*** *on their lawns and fields. Pesticides are chemicals that kill insects. When it rains, the dangerous chemicals are washed into rivers. These chemicals may kill other living things, too.*

Help keep rivers clean!

People must work together to protect rivers. You can help, too! Ask your parents to stop using chemicals that poison rivers. Pick up trash that you find near rivers. Never throw or dump anything harmful into rivers. River water flows, feeds, and gives life on Earth. Ask others to help you take care of it.

These children are pulling trash from a river. They are helping to keep the river near their home clean.

Each one of us has to care about rivers to make sure we have clean water in the future.

Rivers of fun

People love to visit rivers or live near them. Being near rivers makes us feel good. We love to walk on river banks, swim in rivers, paint pictures of rivers, and go fishing, boating, and snorkeling in rivers. Waterfalls are favorite places on rivers. People travel far to see famous waterfalls such as Niagara Falls.

These boys are going to cool off under these cool, fresh waterfalls.

Niagara Falls is made up of two huge waterfalls. They are the American Falls and the Horseshoe Falls. Both are part of the Niagara River. The river creates a border between Canada and the United States. It flows between Lake Erie and Lake Ontario.

Canoeing on a river is great family fun.

This girl has gone snokeling in a river.

These butterflies seem to like rivers, too!

What kind of fish might this boy catch?

Rivers inspire beautiful works of art.

Words to know

Note: Some boldfaced words are defined where they appear in the book.

canal A human-made waterway that connects two areas of water, such as rivers

chemical A substance that is natural or human-made, which may be harmful to living things

continent One of the seven huge areas of land on Earth

current The movement of water in a certain direction

deposit To set down stones, sand, soil, or other materials

fertile Describing land on which many crops grow

fresh water Water that does not contain a lot of salt and is safe to drink

global warming The steady rise in the temperature of Earth's air and waters

ground water Water that is in the ground

hydroelectricity A form of energy made from falling water, which people use for lighting, heating, and running machines

lock An enclosed place on water that allows a ship to be raised or lowered

mouth The place where a river ends

rain forest A thick forest that gets a lot of rain

salt water Water that contains a lot of salt

source The place where a river begins

waterfall A steep drop in a stream or river

Index